PLATFORM PAPERS

QUARTERLY ESSAYS ON THE PERFORMING ARTS FROM CURRENCY HOUSE

No. 44
August 2015

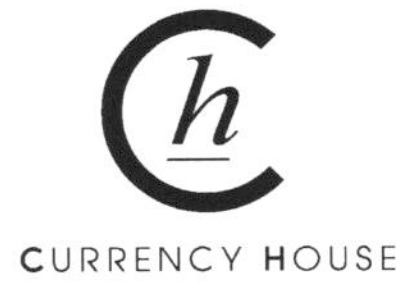

Platform Papers Partners

We acknowledge with gratitude our Partners in continuing support of Platform Papers and its mission to widen understanding of performing arts practice and encourage change when it is needed:

Gillian Appleton
Neil Armfield, AO
Anita Luca Belgiorno Nettis Foundation
Jane Bridge
Katharine Brisbane, AM
Elizabeth Butcher, AM
Penny Chapman
Robert Connolly
Peter Cooke, OAM
Rowena Cowley and Dr Richard Letts, AM
Michael J. Crouch, AO
Ian Enright
Larry Galbraith
Tony Grierson
Gail Hambly
Wayne Harrison, AM
Campbell Hudson
Professors Bruce King and Denise Bradley, AC
Peter Lee
Roderick H. McGeoch, AO
David Marr
Harold Mitchell, AC, AO
Joanna Murray-Smith
Helen O'Neil
Martin Portus
Professor William Purcell
Geoffrey Rush, AC
Dr Merilyn Sleigh
Positive Solutions
Seaborn Broughton Walford Foundation
Sky Foundation
Maisy Stapleton
Augusta Supple
Andrew Upton
Rachel Ward, AM and Bryan Brown, AM
Kim Williams, AM
Professor Di Yerbury, AM

To them and to all subscribers and Friends of Currency House we extend our grateful thanks.

Platform Papers Readers' Forum

Readers' responses to our essays will from now on be posted on our website.

Currency House invites readers to send us considered responses to this or previous Platform Papers in length between 250 and 2000 words. Submissions may be emailed to info@currencyhouse.org.au with a brief biographical note. The Editor welcomes opinion and criticism in the interest of healthy debate but reserves the right to monitor where necessary.

Platform Papers, quarterly essays on the performing arts, are published every February, May, August and November and are available through bookshops, by subscription and on line in paper or electronic version. For details see our website at www.currencyhouse.org.au.

CULTURAL PRECINCTS: ART OR COMMODITY?

JUSTIN MACDONNELL

About the Author

Justin Macdonnell has worked in the arts in Australia and elsewhere for nearly fifty years. He has been employed in arts management, producing and consultancy and has been Director of the Anzarts Institute since 2008. As principal of Macdonnell Promotions (1986-2003) he was one of Australia's leading arts management consultants to the public and private sectors and to scores of arts organisations here and abroad. He is also a poet and librettist and the author of two major works on arts policy.

ACKNOWLEDGEMENTS

I would like to thank Katharine Brisbane and the Board of Currency House for allowing me to produce this paper; Nick Shimmin for his refined and discreet editing and excellent conversation; and Siobhan Lenihan, as always, for her sense, sensibility and eagle eye.

INTRODUCTION

Worldwide, an estimated $US250 billion will be spent in the current decade on creating 'cultural precincts'. In essence, these are collections of buildings and spaces with some arts-related function: museums, galleries, concert halls, theatres. The trend started in the United States in the 1980s and has spread like wildfire. Today, most Australian cities and many towns are building their precinct as urban renewal, tourist destination, residential development and consumer compound tricked out with notions of community engagement, arts promotion and liveability. Does any of it mean anything? There's evidence that more tickets are sold but none that better art is made. Property values rise but are artists better rewarded? The collections of buildings appear grand, but are better connections made than if they were on opposite sides of town? Does the public have a richer experience or just a more convenient one? Are cultural precincts just more commodifying of the arts? Does their very monumental and elite aspect have the contrary effect to the claims made for them?

'A cultural district is a well-recognised, labelled, mixed-use area of a city in which a high concentration of cultural facilities serves as an anchor of attraction.'[1] Others contend more poetically that they have 'the potential to be a vibrant and active place, to be a tourism destination, a cultural Mecca, and an exciting place to live, work and play.'[2] It is a curious and somewhat artificial concept, yet worldwide it has motivated decades of effort and not a little cash in building places of vast economic failure and small artistic success. As Julius Sumner Miller might have asked: Why is it so?[3] The answers are many and not all are encouraging.

I don't intend this essay to be a jeremiad about cultural precincts. First, because there are precincts and precincts and some definitions like those above *are* useful. Second, because even among those that have been created 'top down', by government decree, there's nothing ipso facto objectionable about precincts where, for whatever reason, institutions have been artificially bundled together, even if there is often nothing especially to commend. It's only when extreme rhetoric before the event leads the commentariat to believe that something extraordinary is about to be created that we should begin to question. Or perhaps when, after the event, something remarkable is said to have emerged as a direct result of the precinct itself. I see little evidence anywhere that the latter is so or is ever likely to be.

Essentially, the questions to be asked about cultural precincts are these:

To what extent have such districts ever naturally occurred—or been 'organic' as we are (too) fond of saying now? Or are they always made by bureaucracies for some reason of civic neatness, convenience or to promote a cause? In the end, if they do their job, does it matter how they came to be? That, in turn, raises the further and perhaps most important question: What is their job? And is the ostensible (i.e. publicly proclaimed) intention the real one?

1. The precinct through history

At certain times in history powerful people have caused urban precincts to be created for reasons ranging from the religious to the vainglorious—and often they have been the same. Many, throughout history, have become sites of what today we might regard as 'cultural tourism'. Ancient Delphi is an example. People went there for the good news and adorned the site with thanks if and when they got it. No doubt, as with oracles today, the emission of hot air assisted the process. Maybe some devotees lingered for the Pythian Games which back then rivalled the Olympic. Over in Athens Pericles didn't create the Acropolis but he helped elevate it to what today we understand as a cultural precinct. With its nearby theatre, concert hall and crowning temples it may be regarded as the ancestor of them all. Nonetheless, Socrates preferred to conduct his conversations in what I like to think of as the corner store. Arguably, those conversations have survived better than the Parthenon. Similarly, Augustus may have left Rome a city of marble, but we mostly remember Horace beavering away on his Sabine farm or later Juvenal in his tenement block. Napoleon III caused the Champs-Élysées to be transformed and the Palais Garnier built, but Parisian art and artists stubbornly chose to flourish on the Left Bank. *Sic transit*, as Gloria observed.

Given this history of cultural precincts from the Agora onwards, one of the oddities is that the rhetoric which accompanies the modern version has surprisingly little reference to them as gathering places. Unless you happen to be a dictator there is nothing essentially worrying about a gathering place, but to exclude this role should give our precinct planners pause if among their aesthetic ancestry may be found such unlovely characters as Nero and our old friend Herr Hitler. The manipulation of culture and where it is housed is much loved of tyrants and their ilk, and it is perhaps no accident that the most planned and ordered cultural precinct in Australia (and I happen on balance to think one of the better ones) is Brisbane's South Bank. It was a creature of the Bjelke-Petersen era in the wake of Expo '88 and adorned, if that is the word, with the brutalist concrete architecture of Robin Gibson.

By contrast, a more demotic, higgledy-piggledy Saxon spirit prevailed in London and New York. When comparing the planned to the unplanned, ask yourselves would you rather be in a West End or Broadway theatre (content aside) or in the windswept canyons of (London's) Southbank or the Lincoln Centre? Buenos Aires is a great city of culture not just because, or in spite, of the famed Teatro Colón but because of the viral inter-connectedness of its tango culture in song, dance, visual arts and poetry and in the DNA of its bars and its inhabitants. The art of Paris is least of all the Louvre and the Centre Pompidou and above all still in the studios and cafes. Most would regard Rome as a great locus of culture but its precinct heart is a very big church which may incidentally be a work of art, but only incidentally. Neither Mussolini's faux classical monuments nor his Cinecittá could change that. Beijing's cultural heart lies in the remains of an imperial and Confucian past and no amount of strategic investment in its 'Freeport of Culture' will, in my humble view, add to it any more than the Great Hall of the People has done.

To the extent that cultural locales existed in the past they were of a different order. Activities which might broadly be called 'cultural' occurred in certain places, and structures rose to give effect to them. The town square, piazza or plaza was, if you like, a cultural precinct. There the cathedral, town hall, market place and theatre were accustomed to jostle. Perhaps in time there was a civic palace or government house, courts of law, a parliament, all of which gave expression to a city's 'culture'. Notably, residents bought and sold in the public square and perhaps did their *passeggiata* at dusk, the young fought and made love, politics were debated and on occasion, dissidents were put to death. They were, in short, real places about real things.

But they were there because—like the Piazza della Signoria—they also represented the organs of power and of public discourse as well as concourse. In Anglo-Saxon societies the Town Hall was not just the seat of city government but also hosted lectures and meetings and the gatherings of civil and political society. In Continental Europe and in those countries in the New World that took their tone from there, the municipal theatre or opera house did similar service. Above all, the public went there because there was a serious reason to go. Designed they certainly were, but those historic precincts were not in any sense constructs aimed at luring the public, resident or transient, to a site for some vicarious artistic shopping expedition such as we see all too often in such places today.

Defining terms

So what can we mean today by this term 'cultural precinct'? Many use the words 'precinct', 'district' and 'quarter' interchangeably in this context but there are grounds to make a distinction. A district may reasonably be considered an area in which, for convenience, a sense of togetherness or for some economic reason (e.g. they were located near the railway station or port) a number of complementary activities grew up. The garment district in New York City and the diamond district in Amsterdam are instances. No one planned them, though some were imposed by way of ghettos. For similar reasons, there are or have been districts of booksellers, newspaper publishers and financiers. Fleet Street and Wall Street arose in that way. Precincts or quarters, by contrast, have a sense of official delimiting or design. When we speak of a theatre 'district' we think of bright lights, marquees and post-show buzz on the street and in the nearby bars and restaurants. When we think of 'precincts' the image is of stately edifices and a rather grandly bleak demesne.

Certainly, in appending 'cultural' to a district or a complex we are not usually identifying areas which by historical or other accident may be so labelled for reasons of ethnic identity. The many Chinatowns of this world are good if pedestrian examples. Nor today do we characteristically reference those sites, perhaps heritage listed, which by general agreement have an historical, architectural or environmental merit: Pompeii, Teotihuacán, Angkor Wat, the Kasbah or, closer to home, Port Arthur, Kakadu, Broome, Bendigo. There are complex reasons of culture and identification, positive and negative, that make 'place' of importance to societies large and small, long resident and newly arrived, secure and insecure. But before rushing to sanctify these destinations we should pause to think of them from the outsider's point of view: who finds welcome in them and who might see the situation differently from that of our still very white-bread political and cultural leadership? In a recent paper, Professor Ien Ang of the University of Western Sydney writes that the notion of making some thing or some space a 'home', and perhaps a home strongly guarded, is as old as white settlement. 'The attempt by the European settler/colonist to monopolise the Australian space for the white race had implications for the home-making of another group: Chinese immigrants.'[4] While the idea of Chinatown is now lauded as a measure of our multicultural society, its origins were in the ghettoes despised by the European majority into which the Chinese were crowded as ugly and foreign. We loudly proclaim our diversity and inclusivity from every pulpit but continue to build walls of exclusion higher each day. The same principle may apply to our 'cultural' precincts.

So we may conclude that in this discussion the contemporary cultural precinct is a collection of buildings and the activities they house such as theatres, concert halls, art or other museums, public libraries and so on which have been assembled by government dictate on a site and anointed as 'cultural'. Having settled on this definition, we must ask why these places now seem to deviate so much from the role public precincts have played throughout history. If the idea is safety in numbers, these conglomerates now, rather than corralling the arts for protection against an imagined Visigothic horde, more often fence them against the true life of a city or of engagement in it. By inventing islands of usually 'high' art they do the opposite of what presumably they intend. They make art and artistic expression special, elite and occasional rather than lived in any daily or habitual sense. Too often, they are part of the 'tarting up' by officialdom of sites for what it deems to be 'good' art, mostly to the exclusion of other social practice. They are characterised frequently by monumental architecture, sealed emotionally if not literally against the world where entry requires a code or a special handshake. They become, as Henry James noted, 'those places of which, as their grace of a circumference is nowhere, the dignity of a centre can no longer be predicated.'[5]

2. Australian precincts and exaggerated claims

The fact is that cultural precincts are popping up all over the world now. Each municipal authority wants to have its own. Their motives are many: cultural tourism, urban renewal, crypto-social property development or just a feeling that everyone should have one, like a cricket ground or a leisure centre. Presumably too, municipal leaders believe that such developments dignify their town or city or elevate its concern for the arts by lumping all the arts together, as though mass might somehow equal worth. What, if anything, propels this trend? What, if any, are its benefits? Are the claims made for these behemoths justified? Or are they just another form of contemporary, urban vanity?

We will further examine the rationale of Australia's cultural precincts later in the paper, but let us briefly introduce the most prominent examples. We have seen the burgeoning of 'Banks', notably Melbourne's Southbank and Brisbane's South Bank. These are names slavishly copied from London, like so much of our artificial art, by those who appear ignorant of the significance of the original, or the historical circumstance of the end of World War II which that cluster of halls by the Thames was raised to commemorate. In locating the halls south of the Yarra and Brisbane Rivers respectively our planners were at least geographically accurate; but perhaps it is too much to look for an historical sense in those who believe they can create it artificially.

On the grounds that the arts and heritage have to be housed somewhere, I look at our South Banks and see nothing wrong with them as such. Yet I doubt that I've seen better acting in the Melbourne Theatre Company's flash new premises than I ever did in Russell Street. As a matter of personal preference I'd rather hear the Melbourne Symphony Orchestra in the Melbourne Town Hall and I would sure as hell prefer to hear opera at the St Kilda Palais. By the same token, I'd rather hear the Sydney Symphony Orchestra in the Sydney Town Hall and Opera Australia in the Capitol Theatre. Somehow, I doubt that being in a so-called precinct has ever added one iota to the thrill of a performance or an exhibition beyond what we might have experienced in a stand-alone building, but I suppose we shall never truly know.

Nevertheless, that a mix of state and university officialdom has chosen to group together the Victorian College of the Arts, National Gallery of Victoria, Melbourne Symphony Orchestra, Melbourne Recital Centre, the Australian Ballet, the Melbourne Theatre Company , the Arts Centre venues and not far off the Malthouse seems harmless enough in itself. Or that the local Brisbane powers have situated the Queensland Performing Arts Centre, the State Library, the Queensland Museum, Queensland Art Gallery and GOMA, the Conservatorium, the ABC and not far off the Queensland Theatre Company (QTC), Opera Queensland and Queensland Ballet similarly. I don't know that they talk to each other all that much other than to pass the time of day, but does that matter? In the end it is the conversations of artists not institutions that count. Both these sites have historic entertainment and theatrical associations dating back to the nineteenth century and both are an easy walk from the CBD across a pleasant bridge. If that had been all we meant by cultural precincts I wouldn't have felt the need to write this paper.

To be fair, Melbourne, being Melbourne, has a number of cultural precincts and that, oddly, makes more sense than one grand statement (though as we shall see, Batman's village has that as well). I admit to some bias but feel that truly confident cities have little need of grand plans and precincts. Sydney grew like Topsy and is none the worse for it. It was enlightening to learn at a recent forum in the City Talks series conducted by the City of Sydney that one of the most persuasive suggestions was for better signs and visitor paths to connect the scattered institutions for art and heritage, as has happened in Westminster. It seemed like a reasonable and not too highfalutin' approach.[6]

I'm as happy for governments to invest sensibly in buildings for culture as I am for them to invest in buildings for health, education and public administration. But it is when we are told that these collocations create some magic, cultural chemistry or that a cultural precinct is a place 'where people, ideas and cultural life are nurtured and where infinite experiences unfold … a beacon for culture, diversity, and knowledge' that I begin to question.[7] Infinite experiences? That is a large call. So where then are the works of art that have been forged by all this proximity? Who are the artists claiming to have been nurtured?

In the case of Sydney, what are we to make of such utterances as:

> *Walsh Bay will be an ecosystem for creative production and cultural consumption where innovation and collaboration are a core part of the precinct's operations. This is supported by its design as a visible, networked, hybrid cluster...* [8]

I'm delighted to see the Australian Chamber Orchestra and the Sydney Dance Company make a work together,[9] but I'm guessing it's because Richard Tognetti and Rafael Bonachela had a chat one day over a beer. If propinquity in precincts was as stimulating as claimed, you would think Raf might also have done it with one of the half dozen companies next door to him on the Wharf.

Elsewhere in Australia, the Gold Coast, Lithgow, central Parramatta, and downtown Geelong, to name but the smallest sample, have all acquired or are at risk of acquiring the dubious distinction of a precinct. Adelaide boasts its North Terrace strip and plans to remodel its Riverbank; Perth's 'Creative Quarter' is reuniting neglected East Perth/Northbridge with the CBD. There are also prominent examples throughout the Commonwealth: Johannesburg, for example, has been struggling with its own Cultural 'Quarter' for more than a decade. Its vision boldly states:

> *Newtown will become the creative capital of Johannesburg and South Africa: dynamic, vibrant, sophisticated, and cosmopolitan, boasting the best cultural offerings in Africa... [attracting] new private sector (and other) investment to complement and enhance the facilities and programme already available in the cultural quarter as a destination center and desired location for the creative industries.*[10]

Sadly, it has been slow to prosper. Likewise, Auckland has been wrestling with the development of the site of its former Civic Administration being cheek by jowl with the already very active Aotea Centre and its neighbours. 'This will create an arts and entertainment hub with subsequent opportunity for associated commercial and retail activity.'[11] But not, it seems, just yet.

One can't help feeling that these plans and their precincts are just too neat: too ordered and too antiseptic. For all the alleged advantages of setting diverse practices together I question whether any more collaboration has happened among the artists in these places than might have happened had they met accidentally in a cafe or a toilet block. Where such things occur, they do so between individuals, not institutions or buildings elegantly or inelegantly parked side by side. What they also overlook is that 85 per cent of creative and cultural enterprise is small business for which these monsters mean little and to which they contribute not at all. None of this is to suggest that cultural and creative endeavour is not crucial to cities. The question is whether there is evidence that the presence of these islands of grandeur is adding to that.

Yet these exaggerated goals for the cultural conglomerate are writ large all over the country and all over the world. That would be fine if there were demonstrable economies of scale, cheaper tickets, more outreach and education or even greater ease of public access. Who would quarrel with that? But in fact, what we see is growth by 'visitation' and art calibrated by economic impact.

3. The institutions and their policies

It is perhaps not surprising in a world where international bodies are created to ease our souls and negotiate our baser urges that an institution should have been established to take charge of all this pretentiousness. Known as the Global Cultural Districts Network (GCDN), it is an association of centres of arts and culture worldwide that promotes 'co-operation and knowledge-sharing among those responsible for conceiving, funding, building, and operating cultural districts'. It has been claimed rather extravagantly by its begetters that 'cultural infrastructure projects play a significant role in nation-building and urban development'[12] But do they? It may well be argued that the Parthenon was the highest 'infrastructural' achievement of fifth century BCE Athens and without doubt it kicked along the city's 'urban development'. However, I think that rowing in the navy at the Battle of Salamis or being in the chorus of a play by Aeschylus were more likely to have forged the Attic 'right stuff'.

The GCDN's executive director asserts that 'They encourage visitors and residents, young and old, to intermingle in ways that destratify, desegregate and generally democratise.'[13] Rendering society more democratic is an admirable aim, but it is far from clear who or what may be destratified in these endeavours or in what sense the people may be desegregated. How these goals are to be achieved by creating enclaves of this kind we can only speculate. GCDN goes on to explain that 'long-term demand may be a subordinate consideration in planning compared with the political priority afforded these overarching goals'.[14] Albert Speer might have shared those sentiments but I doubt that today's artists would applaud. GCDN adds, somewhat meekly in the circumstances: 'This, in turn, means that strategic investment in audience development, marketing, and programming *may* be all the more important'[my emphasis].[15] If I understand this correctly, they are saying that while politics takes precedence in these matters, we may have to tack on some audience-friendly art to dress it up. It will come then as no surprise to learn that one of the Network's founding members is the Barangaroo project in Sydney. But perhaps the most jejune of GCDN's utterances is the following:

> *Globalization has led to competition between cities and regions for inward investment, knowledge workers, and tourists. Large-scale cultural projects are now an increasingly important driver of competitiveness and are key in branding and differentiating regions and cities.*[16]

This is the clearest statement that these precincts are in fact culture reduced to a branding exercise. In an age when arts grants characteristically require a business plan, none of this is perhaps so very surprising.

In summary, GCDN suggests there are 'common

agenda' for these ventures around the world. The management verbiage alone probably says it all about the aims and objectives of those who propagate this guff, but for the record they include:

- Content and programming strategies;
- The development of strategic alliances to share content;
- Cultural project management;
- Segmented strategies for development of key audience groups and subsequent marketing (local communities, tourists);
- Marketing, branding and identity;
- The development of education and outreach programs that enable meaningful relationships between the cultural districts and the wider communities in which they are located; and
- Recruitment and training of staff across a range of operational skills, and in particular, curatorial, programming, production, customer service and front of house, and fundraising; and
- The effective integration of technology.[17]

Two more tendencies are at work in this area which seem to have profound implications for public arts policy. The first is the urge to build splendacious theatres and concert halls not on city streets where theatre and cinemas were once to be found, but on inaccessible points of land, on riverbanks or in parks, in any event as far as possible from the normal passing parade. The second is the passion for recycling old buildings, and here the dreaded 'urban renewal' rears its head. When they have outlived their usefulness as post office, customs house, power station or wharf, these are converted, often at greater cost than to build something new, into an 'arts facility' where for heritage reasons not enough can be altered to make them genuinely useful but just enough can be done to make them plausible. Sydney's Museum of Contemporary Art in the art deco former harbourmaster's building is an egregious example of this folly.

As far back as 2001 observers were raising cautionary notes for cultural district development. For example, one paper noted astutely that

> *the link between cultural districts and economic growth was and is far from established, and the urban revitalization effected by cultural districts may lead to a process of inner-city gentrification which is not simply of itself always desirable … [First], the defence of a district for the cultural environment it provides is not the same as the defence of a district for its economic growth properties. Second, not all of the possible goals are mutually compatible. Certain commercial innovations might stimulate growth yet denigrate the cultural environment; and not all urban renewal schemes lead to increased growth.*[18]

This policy also assumes that 'arty' people like old things or that we and our public will be content with second best. If enough old buildings are unsuitably converted into 'arts spaces' (as though vacuity were of itself a boon) hey presto, we have a precinct. As they are old and deserted, so they are often in what are now inaccessible locations. By contrast, how much more convenient in every way is the purpose built Sydney Recital Hall right in the middle of the CBD, five minutes from virtually every rail and bus line (and soon tram line) in the city. In contrast, at the Sydney Opera House or on Hickson Road, no bus comes and you can die waiting for a cab.

Of all the many dreadful cities I have visited or lived in over the decades my prize for the worst goes to Brasília, Brazil's artificial capital created by decree in the 1950s. This is 'precinct' on a vast scale. True, it has Niemeyer's shimmering white concrete buildings as consolation and an ordered pattern to put chessboards to shame, but there everything is subdivided: a parliamentary district, a diplomatic district, a shopping district and of course a cultural district, all laid out (as Bobby Helpmann said of his native Adelaide), like a cemetery and each impermeable to the other. It's an extreme example, to be sure, but serves as a reductio ad absurdum of where such civic planning can lead. Brasília gives the lie to the GCDN's unsubstantiated claim that precincts 'destratify, desegregate and generally democratise'. However, our city planners continue the trend, insisting on enhanced 'liveability'.

Added to this, I see these precincts as representing an abandonment of all commercial instinct which previously drove the siting of theatres and other cultural institutions. It is now left entirely to government or quasi-government agencies; we have lost any truly robust informed public patronage in favour of what John Armstrong has called 'an astonishing corruption of consciousness practised upon us by a decadent cultural elite'.[19] Decision-making now seems dominated by a desire to put the arts in a gilded cage where they can do no harm, and yet the claims made on their behalf continue to be extreme.

Business deals and building projects

What then, as Mr Lenin might have asked, is to be done? The City of Sydney recently undertook a massive exercise aimed at the creation of a cultural plan. In many ways the process has been exemplary as to the range of consultation, seriousness of engagement with both practitioners and concerned members of the public and in the time and energy devoted to it by the elected officials. Above all, it has demonstrated the importance of local government as regulator and giver of consent for change and development. More than grant programs, staging festivals and events and enlivening streetscapes, it is about how government can persuade or, if you prefer, compel developers to reshape their plans to meet social and cultural needs. Normally, contemplation of the Barangaroo fiasco would not make one very sanguine about this prospect. But perhaps the best way to break with the trend of precinct agglomeration is to provide alternatives and the best impulse to alternatives is still likely to be the market. Property developers have an odd tendency to put buildings where they believe they can make a buck. This is a compelling reason why the inclusion of theatres, halls, galleries and studios in real buildings situated in diverse places in a city and inhabited by real people, either at work or at home, is greatly to be preferred to cultural gulags on the periphery. Again, the

Sydney Recital Hall is a prime example (the MLC Theatre Royal is admittedly a less happy one). If that trend were to be encouraged, even enforced, maybe the public will vote with their feet, the producers and promoters make money, the arts bloom on highways and byways and the politicians will see the folly of their precinct ways.

Intriguingly, one of the few projects in Australia that actually took that path is in suburban Sydney. Willoughby Council's Concourse precinct in Chatswood includes the municipal library, two performance venues, a small exhibition space, conference facilities and a jumbo screen *á la* Melbourne's Federation Square. It has not been without its teething problems. But its starting point was at least predicated on situating the precinct in the heart of its commercial district, five minutes walk from a major rail and bus interchange. It is opposite a Westfield shopping mall and thus fulfils the criterion of being where people have occasion to go. Chatswood library is held to be one of the busiest in NSW, so there is daytime traffic as well as night-time attendance. Above all perhaps, its economic model (if we may use that crude term) is built around a suite of 12 rent-paying restaurants, shops and other businesses, including a bank and a medical centre, which cross-subsidises the whole. It may not be perfect, but it beats putting these facilities in a beautiful but isolated leafy setting where no one need ever go.[20]

But here's a quirky thought: perhaps rather than building these fancy environs, what about taking the arts to the precincts that already exist? If we aim to have supermarkets of the arts and are genuinely looking for new locations, wouldn't it be preferable to take the arts to the shopping malls? Now, many will argue that the shopping mall is dead and in the US, harbinger of consumer sentiment, that may well be true (though that doesn't seem to have stopped record US takeover bids for shopping centres here). But in Australia, a quick saunter through Chadstone, Chermside, Macquarie Park or Penrith Plaza on a weekday morning would change your mind. They are genuinely places of concourse and discourse. The shopping mall is also booming in India and China where, let us recall, most people on earth live. For shopping malls are by no means just for shopping. Shopping at the mall is a social experience. According to a recent survey of more than 3,400 adults ages 18 and up, 81 percent of Americans go shopping with another person. The inaugural survey, designed to understand why people come to the mall, was released by Glimcher Retail Trust. Despite today's time-deprived culture, the study showed that people are willing to drive up to 30 minutes to get to the mall and stay one to five hours on a monthly basis. The research found that

> *the mall continues to be the central gathering place in almost every community. Farmers' markets and live music were among the top events shoppers would like to see on a more regular basis at the mall, followed by community events and classes. Similarly, 52 percent of people surveyed said if stores offered more experiences like yoga classes, cooking demos or workshops, they would visit the mall more frequently.*[21]

What's more, the public is already accustomed to find

entertainment at shopping malls. Not only do people go there to shop both for their necessities and their fripperies, but they also go for relaxation.

> *There are movies, sometimes as many as fifteen or sixteen. In addition, arcades are available for children, teens and adults. Some parents drop their children off at the arcade, give them a roll of quarters and pick them up after they have completed their shopping. For the hungry shopper there is a food court, which provides fast food for those shoppers who want to relax and possibly have a cocktail with their meal, other restaurants are available. The mall even offers concerts, outings and other events, especially during the holiday periods.*[22]

Are the arts just missing out here? Hoyts and their ilk seem to have got the message some time back, one of many indicators that it may be wise to 'think before you precinct'.

But to return drearily to the new world order, our friends at the GCDN, quoted earlier, state that there are some 70 precinct developments currently across the globe representing about $US250 billion in investment. Now it must be said that on inspection that figure, like some of their other claims, proves a little wobbly. It appears to include a great deal of cultural infrastructure including new arts building of one kind or another that may or may not in the long run form part of some identifiable cultural 'zone'. What is clear, however, is that an overwhelming amount of this is public investment or public-private co-venture, though making these distinctions is increasingly difficult and the real nature of public investment harder to untangle in some jurisdictions than in others. To take an entirely hypothetical case: an arts complex is being built in an emirate by private investment but the private company is owned by the Emir's nephew. How do we classify that? Probably arbitrarily and perhaps it doesn't matter. I have long been intrigued by what for want of a better expression I shall call the 'Abu Dhabi phenomenon', that is to say the sight of astonishing twenty-first century cities rising overnight from barren land. I have wondered to what extent the urge to build them—complete, it should be noted, with opera houses and art museums—reflects the world of Scheherezhade where jewel-encrusted palaces appear overnight from the desert sands peopled by benevolent rulers and impossibly beautiful odalisques. Are we all perhaps infected with that Arabian dream?

If we are, in so dreaming we may be dooming ourselves to imitating or even benefitting from the practices of blatantly undemocratic and often repressive regimes and their vanity projects. The local populace has no influence in shaping these schemes and, it is reasonable to suppose, only limited ability to access them. And do not for one moment think that amid all the dreaming this isn't also big business. Sinbad and his crew were always in it for the loot; along with building the Parthenon, Pericles kept a treasury on Delos; Delphi had seven; at base the Medici were bankers—for all its fine art collection, Uffizi means 'offices' and those rooms were the Wall Street of their day. The link between art and mammon has always been strong in ruling circles. As well, where there are 'issues' there will be consultants and where consultants, networks—and it follows as night does day that international conferences will be *de rigeur*. Precinct experts go about as ravening lions, meeting to discuss in depth something that may not truly exist. But what undoubtedly does exist in these great schemes is that taxpayers get to underwrite the loss-leading side of the deal (the cultural infrastructure) and the developers' investment, usually with significant concessions, is directed to the profitable aspect (car parking, residential towers, hotels, casinos). Rarely has anyone planned that the profits of the latter should sustain the content of the former.

The GCDN is, of course, governed by an advisory board and is supported by its members. We are told it is the first forum to exist for those responsible for these projects in which they can 'analyse and solve their common challenges, the scope for collaboration and evolving practice'.[23] It is rather as though they believe it to be a form of cultural naturopathy. As Lawrence Durrell so presciently observed as long ago as 1974, 'The art form of the age is not the diary any more but the case history'.[24]

The GCDN, it is important to know, is sponsored by 'the New Cities Foundation, Dallas Arts District, and AEA Consulting' and 'serves to support the leaders of cultural districts—both planned and existing—internationally'. It provides the following services for its members:

> *Regular convening to share emerging best practices, hear expert panels, and discuss the place of cultural districts in urban policy, economic development,*

and related areas of public policy such as travel and tourism; original research on topics of common interest such as programming, audience development, cultural tourism, professional development, relevant trends in technology and creative industries strategies; regular summaries and circulation of secondary research and news of common interest; virtual forums for detailed sharing of information and discussion of opportunities and challenges; and opportunities for establishing strategic partnerships for content, programming, skills training, and knowledge transfer.[25]

Of course, in the horse trading that takes place in many of these developments, sometimes society *is* a winner. There are cases where the acquisition, sale or consolidating of sites by public authorities destined for cultural purposes may directly or indirectly offer new opportunities like affordable housing, child care and recreation facilities and a range of social goodies that add to the quality of life. These are, of course, claimed as spin-offs from the precinct and lauded as such, rightly or wrongly. As to whether the same 'outcomes', as we are keen to describe them, would have been achieved had the government in question chosen to build something else, such as a school or hospital, is never seriously canvassed. To each according to his need, as someone said.

We have noted that over the next decade hundreds of billions will be invested in the creation of these new cultural districts around the world. Since that is so, clearly the arguments put forward have been persuasive to many who are not otherwise easily parted from their money.[26] A successful cultural district, it is said quite without irony, is not just one that is built, but one that, once built, thrives and, in thriving, animates the city or region that it serves. Equally clearly, this all-embracing definition of 'success' has been crucial to persuading tight-fisted local government in liberal democracies, value-conscious Chinese bureaucrats and prodigal Arabian princes to cough up. Just as clearly, it has been central to those like the GCDN who benefit from what I fear may already be called the cultural precinct industry. 'Success' they proudly proclaim, 'is not just getting an arts building or series of buildings out of the ground, it is about ensuring that they are viable and play a central role in their communities.'[27] What these advocates may lack in subtlety they make up for in blandness.

Few would contest the view that 'cultural' buildings such as art museums, theatres, concert halls and the like have played a role in shaping the identity of some cities. But most genuine entertainment and arts areas grew by accident. Indeed, in the case of London and New York they thrive almost antithetically to any civic plan and have done so over the course of centuries and mercifully quite without any public or private strategy other than human convenience. The precinct pushers would argue that today cultural infrastructure is increasingly planned large-scale and top down. They quote Saadiyat Island in Abu Dhabi, Beijing's Olympic Green, the Dallas Arts District, Chicago's Millennium Park, Hong Kong's West Kowloon Cultural District, Singapore's Esplanade, and Doha's Cultural District as models of how high-profile urban developments have been planned 'to embrace cultural activities as an important part of the public realm'.[28] Perhaps they could have taken Alexandria as their model. That is a town devised for precinct propaganda if ever there was one! That it 'invented' the library they would no doubt have labelled 'win-win'.

Yet even these advocates are sufficiently self-aware to notice that such projects are 'difficult to get right, and expensive and politically embarrassing to get wrong'.[29] In fact, to date it's hard to quote an instance of the former anywhere on earth, while recent history is littered with examples of the latter or where the results are, if not bad, at best indifferent. In what may be the understatement of our time, they also note that these projects require 'a great deal of expertise across a range of disciplines'.[30] Notwithstanding, there are scores of them worldwide either in planning stages or actually under construction, and that is in addition to those completed in the past twenty years.

The GCDN believes that the reasons for this global trend are not difficult to find and nominates nation building and global competition as among them. However, these are scarcely plausible explanations, given that this ambition is more easily achieved by having the tallest building, the most lavish hotel and the largest football stadium. For the truth we must look elsewhere. Overwhelmingly, the instances cited are of developments which have clear commercial elements such as casinos and showbiz arenas and are located in countries which have at best a tangential historical or cultural association with the art forms or traditions they are intended to house. The fact is that there is no market dimension to any of those arts in these countries. There is attendance yes, but sales no. The shrewder minds who contemplate the explosion of venues in China today will readily tell you that as long as the government gives tickets away en masse as *panem et circenses*, there will never be a market. We are deluding ourselves as they are deluding themselves. At best we are witnessing enclave economies of art.

4. Australia and precinct policy

One could have a long and somewhat diagnostic discussion about some of the major precinct developments infecting Australia's creative landscape, but to what end? Perhaps it would be more instructive to look at what we say to the world about our own capabilities in this area and what that is worth. A recent publication *Cultural Precincts* produced by Austrade is telling in this respect, in particular as to the lack of clarity about what we are really promoting to a world purportedly eager to devour our skills.[31]

As with the GCDN, the confusion extends to the very terms used. The booklet is subtitled 'Creative Expertise delivering world class cultural venues'. Given that this *is* Austrade, for which otherwise I have great respect, it understandably focuses on making a sales pitch about the quality of Australian design and construction and to a lesser degree the management and consulting services which we might offer to potential clients in other countries (notably, one assumes, in Asia). However, the equation of 'venues' with 'precincts' and the lack of rigour as to the distinction between them reveals much. The pitch focuses, perhaps not unreasonably, on architectural distinction as well as on 'managing world-leading cultural institutions'.

No attention is paid to why we might choose to create these places, still less what experience Australia has to offer our neighbours in making this claim. Nor is any evidence offered that we have expertise in turning such hubs of art from building sites to thriving, creative locations.

In that context, it is especially instructive when it comes to identifying our supposed international leadership. Four performing arts identities are listed: Michael Lynch, Jonathan Mills, Craig Hassall and Timothy Walker. Now I am sure none of them, worthy as they all are in other areas of their genuine expertise, will object if I point out that only one, namely Lynch, has actually managed or presided over a multi-venue building project. None as far as I know has 'animated a precinct', though it could be argued that directing international festivals may have given Mills some insights. In fact, the entire document in its 43 lavishly illustrated pages fails to address any of the issues of 'precinct' as opposed to 'venue'. It is of course a promotional tract and no one wants to ruin a good promotion by raising tricky issues of substance. Don't misunderstand me, I am all for spruiking our skills and talents abroad. We are well placed, if on occasion a little naïve, about our capacity to export them to Asia. But at times this pamphlet feels as though we are feeding a cargo cult, and however profitable in the short term, in the long term they usually come to grief.

So by weary steps we come to the *Melbourne Arts Precinct Blueprint*. For a process that seemingly cost $900,000, the resultant 'blueprint' was a tawdry little essay awash with jargon and third-hand corporatese: 'there has been an absence of a shared vision for the area, partially due to the lack of a dedicated precinct marketing plan'.[32] So what's lacking is a marketing plan? Silly us! When a reasonable reader might have thought that what was absent was a soul. This document of blithering idiocy goes on to suggest that

> *an online 'one-stop shop' and networked mobile platform would engage audiences in new ways, producing information about Arts Precinct programs, activities and wayfinding [sic] through a single access point.*

Many, including those who dwell with great skill and effectiveness within the perimeters of Southbank, have taken up the cudgels on this matter. Among the most vociferous has been Leon van Schaik, Professor of Architecture at RMIT, who took particular exception in an article flagged as 'Street life doesn't come from precinct thinking'.[33] He asked what evidence there was that an arts precinct was in any way a desirable thing for a city to have.

> *This smacks of the 'let's tidy up the city' thinking of planners from the mid-twentieth century. Thanks to them, cities around the world are encumbered with problematic arts ghettos, constantly sucking in public monies as they struggle (as this blueprint does) to 'bring life' 'night and day' to their open spaces. Such precinct thinking is engulfing central Melbourne, and the Sports Precinct, for example, grows ever more isolated from any 'life' other than that of major events.*[34]

He also noted the blueprint's sneering at the 'inward looking institutions' that compete to provide access to peak experiences in the arts. The authors of this report then

> *segue to depictions of an area transformed into 'life'. But 'life' as depicted in this blueprint, including 'New Orleans style jazz bands' is something plucked from elsewhere and programmed by some apparatchik and delivered into the streets and spaces on a 'rolling program' of consumable entertainment.*[35]

In his fulmination about the waste of money that might otherwise have been spent on making real art, he asks a critical question: 'Is this really a government matter? Although this report uses the Maoist phrase calling for the blooming of a hundred flowers, here as in China governments aren't good at this…'[36] And nor, we might add, have they ever been. Other critics shared his views.[37]

'Animate' is a word much used in the language of precincts. It reminds us of the 'vibrancy' so beloved of arts funding and often linked to the notion that if you put them all together, great and wonderful collaborations will flow. In fact, experience suggests no such thing and here it is important to make a further distinction. In any district, precinct, quarter, it is possible to organise events every week or month or year. Whoever or whatever coordinates the area can book an activity and place it in any nook or cranny and thereby they will 'animate' the place if animate is interpreted as 'fill'. Sufficiently well promoted, the event may attract a crowd. Prominent and expensive enough, it might well attract a crowd from far afield. But rarely if ever does this come about from a spontaneous upsurge of the collaborative spirit.

Melbourne's Summersalt Festival in 2015 was a case in point. No doubt a sign of things to come, billed as collaboration among the constituent organisations of Southbank and presented within its perimeters, it was a mix of work from hither and yon, staged as with any festival within a given locale. To be fair, there were some works produced by the resident companies, such as MTC's *Cybec Electric* (which it would probably be doing anyway, as it has before) and notably work by the VCA students and staff. But there were virtually no collaborations between the institutions or certainly no more than might have occurred had organisations located at opposite ends of Swanston Street or even in other cities chosen to get together. As had been predicted by van Schaik it was, in fact, a jamboree to cheer up the area for summer and nothing wrong with that. But let us not pretend it was the result of those companies living artistically cheek by jowl. Of that there is scant evidence.

Brisbane can boast a similar recent example. Desiring to have 'animation' that would embrace all the institutions lining South Bank from GOMA to the Queensland Conservatorium, it was decided to have a Valentine's Day Guinness World Record-breaking busking event. Now with galleries, museums, libraries and theatres and their many and genuinely charming adjacent spaces in the mix, one might have thought that each resident institution could have striven to ensure those buskers reflect in interesting and original ways the nature of their arts or artefacts to the greater glory and edification of all. Sadly, not so. In fact, while myriads of buskers sang and strummed and otherwise exercised their diverse crafts all over South Bank sufficiently to break the record, making it happen was just hard work for a small band of Brisbane Festival organisers. It was, in short, an event or festival by any other name and might just as well have run the length of Queen Street or at the 'Gabba for all the artistic collaboration it entailed among the denizens of South Bank.

These stories can be replicated everywhere there is a cultural precinct. When from time to time those who co-ordinate such places are panicked into the realisation that nothing is happening in them other than what might be happening were their constituent elements situated on opposite sides of town, a festival is born. It may not matter that it is so if the public enjoys the result, but we should not delude ourselves that something mysterious and osmotic is occurring because a theatre company, art museum and symphony orchestra occupy the same city block.

The Brisbane cultural precinct is billed as the centrepiece of Queensland's arts portfolio. It occupies a prime location on Brisbane's South Bank, adjacent to the city's CBD and as we noted earlier, it is home specifically to all the state's leading arts and cultural institutions. This collection of so many co-located cultural institutions on a single site is held to be unique in Australia and rare worldwide, and that may be. Beyond doubt, it represents a major investment by the government as well as the ABC and Griffith University and it's said to be loved by locals and tourists alike with around five million visiting each year, which many still attribute to the hangover effect of Expo '88 thirty years ago. Given what we have seen so far, it will come as no surprise to learn that there is a master plan for the cultural precinct which, when complete, will provide 'the strategic vision and implementation plan' to guide development and investment in the precinct for the next 20 years. Somewhat gnomically, an official statement advising of this goes on to make the dubious claim that 'global trends indicate that there is a growing appetite *for authentic cultural experiences*' [my emphasis].[38] It adds that two challenges for the Master Plan will be 'defining these experiences and how the cultural precinct will continue to provide these opportunities in the future'.[39] Greater minds than those working on this proposal have, I fear, tried to capture 'authentic cultural experience' before today. We, and the good taxpayers of Brisbane, may have to wait a while for that one.

Nevertheless,

> *a core objective of the Queensland Government's cultural precinct Strategy 2013-2015 is for the master plan to maximise the return on public investment that this unique co-location offers to the people of Queensland. In turn, the cultural precinct will grow Queensland's arts and cultural sector and unlock the potential of cultural tourism.*[40]

Well, there you have it: a precinct to grow the sector and unlock the potential. But what is latent in this, as in so many grand schemes, is an unspoken risk—namely that of harnessing creative endeavour as a workhorse of tourism. For that is not an inert relationship. It has the power to distort the thing it seeks to celebrate, just as all tourism may be held to damage the very thing that attracts its sightseers. It is the ultimate commodification of value when tourism steps beyond being a companion in promoting the arts to being that which determines what it is, how it is represented to the public and finally and most frighteningly what it is permitted to say. Brisbane has a magnificent collection of institutions, of which GOMA is rightly held to be outstanding. But if the motivation for locating them in a cultural precinct is to make the institutions an engine of tourism, one fears for the value of the artistic production that their proximity is intended to encourage.

Meanwhile, the spirit of the times is just as alive in the West. Perth's Creative Quarter is about

> *creating a network of exciting destinations and places throughout the city and across the metropolitan area. Considerable investment by both the public and private sectors in recent years has attracted unique small bars and restaurants to the CBD, exciting new retail and cultural experiences and a calendar of events that are encouraging people to rediscover our city.*[41]

Leading the charge of this urban regeneration is the Perth Cultural Centre. Home to the state's most significant cultural and learning institutions, this precinct has 'undergone significant transformation to become one o

Perth's premier events destinations and a favourite meeting place'. The West Australian Government—through the Metropolitan Redevelopment Authority and the Department of Culture and the Arts—has invested more than $35 million into the precinct over the past four years to address the area's 'negative reputation as a place synonymous with antisocial behaviour'. Which means, one supposes, that such roaring boys as Christopher Marlowe and Brendan Behan would not be welcome there.

> *The vision was to create a place where people of all ages and backgrounds could interact, to attract new groups of people—particularly families and children—into the city and encourage Australians to rediscover the cultural heart of Perth.* [42]

I'm sure it was with the best of intentions that this statement was made to sound like Kindergarten of the Air. It goes on:

> *What was unique about this project was the approach to planning and design. The Perth Cultural Centre precinct had all the 'building blocks' of a great place—the museum, art gallery, independent theatre groups and other wonderful cultural institutions.* What was missing was activity in the open areas. [my emphasis].[43]

Where in all of this is risk? Adventure? Brinkmanship? Whatever the reality may be, it is dismaying that those who shape the destinies of such places have nothing to say of them that is not platitudinous and accommodating to the lowest common denominator. Surely the public would have more fun at Waterworld?

Back in Queensland we are told that the Gold Coast cultural precinct will be a place where people come together to engage with arts, culture and each other. The precinct will provide a platform from which arts contributors and visitors alike can discover, share and create. As the Gold Coast matures, it is alleged 'the precinct will be a focal point to reflect on our cultural heritage as we continue to shape our sense of self as a city'.[44] So far, so good. At least it sounds vigorous. However, as we move on we discover a somewhat confusing string of mixed metaphors in which the 'vision' for the Gold Coast cultural precinct

> *tells the story of a dynamic, seamless interaction between indoor and outdoor experiences. In an arts and culture corridor that is distinctly Gold Coast, civic gardens will interface with a new arts museum and performing arts centre. The precinct will be activated through a rich and ever-changing artistic program and energised by cafes and restaurants, production studios and showrooms for arts and creative industries.*[45]

The City Council held a global design competition to deliver this landmark precinct which has resulted in 'a colourful vertical Art Tower, expanded performing arts facilities and stunning outdoor Artscape. [...] together with integrated allied uses, generating 24-hour activity and excitement'. The pitch goes on to say that 'we must ensure the cultural precinct we deliver is a must-see destination for residents and visitors and a place where pivotal moments in our city's life take place.' This at least is a rare acknowledgment that these places may have some gathering function, but since this is—typically—located far from where people now choose to gather for other purposes, in a city which to date has not developed a heart, we might wonder if the ambition is achievable.

Nonetheless, I dwell on this instance because it is still in the making. Work on its first stage commences in early 2016. Stage 1 is expected to be completed before the city hosts the Gold Coast 2018 Commonwealth Games™. One can but wish them well and hope it has the transforming effect for which the city so clearly hopes. History is not, however, on their side.

5. Overseas ambition and the business case

But all these plots and plans are as chickenfeed compared to the mighty works envisaged by our Ozimandias neighbours. In China alone, the pace of urban growth since 2001 has been equivalent to building a new Singapore each month for the past 12 years. This reflects even greater shifts around the world as an estimated 100 million people a year move from rural to urban areas. Increasingly, these new urban areas are also the major global producers of wealth and economic growth. Mind you, at least some of the Chinese urban explosion may prove illusory.[46] In the face of these facts, we can have sympathy with the panic that drives governments to give the resultant megacities a soul. But as Faustus showed, souls are not an easily tradable commodity and when they are traded it usually ends in tears.

Now plans are afoot to create a new $800 million, tax-free arts and entertainment hub in Beijing in the hope of giving the country's gradually growing culture industries a jolt. The so-called 'Beijing Freeport of Culture' is the brainchild of the Beijing Gehua Cultural Development Group, a company owned by the Beijing municipal government. Located next to Beijing Capital Airport, the tax-free culture zone will include film and television production facilities, fine arts storage and offices for companies involved in a range of creative businesses from luxury goods to software design.[47] Gehua's ambition is to plant the seeds for a culture-industry hotbed in the Chinese capital that boasts elements of Hollywood, Silicon Valley and New York's Chelsea District all in one commercial compound. The company hopes to attract upward of 50 companies—half of them foreign, half domestic —to do $8 billion (50 billion yuan) worth of business at the Freeport by 2016. Such specially designated tax-free economic zones were integral in China's opening up to global capitalism in the 1980s and 90s, when demarcated business districts were set up in the southern city of Shenzhen and the Pudong section of Shanghai to foster the country's then-nascent manufacturing sector. But this will be the first time China is attempting to implement the tax-free, infrastructure investment model of 'economic zones' to facilitate growth in the less predictable arts and culture sector. Here at least the commercial factor is upfront, but it is in fields of artistic production where the market has long dominated the scene.

Whether these developments anywhere on earth are new or newly formed (perhaps from a mix of old buildings and new), they are usually enveloped by spirited language about cultural development, housing the arts and making the world a better place. But it is never long before the economic determinant enters and talk turns to tourist dollars and the night-time economy and gross value and the multiplier effect of cultural activity on such and such a place. None of that is wrong in itself, but if the intention is to create a cultural supermarket where one and all can bring and buy, perhaps it would be more honest just to say so.

Adrian Ellis, director of the GCDN and AEA Consulting, acknowledges at least that successful cultural districts are powerful policy tools. His prose may be opaque but the meaning somehow seeps through:

For planners, [cultural districts] can help build community and social capital; for sociologists, they keep at bay the forces of anomie; for economists, they incubate and inculcate creativity, and draw those fickle high-net-worth tourists; and for the politicians and the semioticians alike, they signify and calibrate complex aspirations and identities.

And like much else in the world today, it is driven by numbers:

Opinion polls of what makes a liveable city have a real impact on public policy. Global competition between cities for highly mobile capital and skilled labour has put culture and creativity, and the infrastructure that supports them, near the front of the queue for public investment. If this investment is made intelligently, the significant proportion of the world's population that is living in new cities has at least the prospect of one important dimension of a liveable life.[48]

Clearly many have been swayed by these quasi-corporate arguments that seem to say cultural precincts and all that goes with them are self-evidently good. Business cases have been advanced (though rarely adequately tested) that they offer civic, social, economic and of course cultural benefits. If the level of investment quoted earlier is a guide, many have bought the business case. Whether from conviction, delusion or cynicism we cannot be sure, though we might hazard a guess that it is a mix of all three. None of this is to say that occasionally, even if by accident, these ventures may turn out okay. On the grounds that even Hollywood can sometimes create art there is no *prima facie* reason to suppose that a 'created' cultural precinct could not work. It's just that it's hard to think of one that does. Anyone who has stood on the freezing plaza of Lincoln Centre (arguably the blueprint of them all) or worse, the windswept canyons of the Los Angeles Music Center, will have surely asked themselves: was this a good idea? Isn't it in every way more agreeable to go to a theatre around Times Square?

6. CONCLUSION

In drawing these threads together to grasp the real nature of the cultural precinct in Australia and where policymakers should look in the coming century, I really want to ask a deeper question about the nature of cultural imitation, or perhaps cultural contagion is a better way to put it. On the one hand, as I view it from Australia (and of course this question must inevitably look very different from other parts of the globe) I wonder how much has our deep-seated imitative mentality shaped what we are doing and saying about this phenomenon. Is the precinct in the New World about cultural envy of the Old? If so, surely it's time we got over it. The cultural precincts of Europe are what they are, either for reasons of faith, pride or accident, often all three. We cannot by design reproduce any of these other than perhaps the pride.

Is there a kind of reverse engineering at work here which connects the curious Austrade publication, referred to above, with these oddly situated and seemingly alien cultural devices? Is it the case that, after looking at some egregious cases in the West, the East wants them? And that Australia, in a curious halfway house between the two, feels the need to demonstrate that we can answer the need and so retroactively start to build? Having neither the funds nor the political will to build the Pyramids, have we, as it were, settled perhaps for a rather suburban and possibly unwarranted mastaba?

Some years ago I was wandering about the Yale campus in New Haven. Those of you who know it or other Ivy League colleges will recall how strenuously they try to imitate in neo-Gothic style the Oxbridge colleges (as, in a half-hearted way, our 'sandstone' universities also tried to do). Yale and others persisted well into the twentieth century with this folly. Above all, the problem is that they are too perfect, so unlike the source of their imitation which is an often random mix of mediaeval, Tudor and what you will. They are frozen in a time that has little to do with America and as a result have become almost a caricature of the very thing they set out to worship. Paradoxically, they became an abrogation of the spirit of severance from Europe to which the US founding fathers aspired. As I contemplated this envy of the old, I wondered whether, in varying degrees, some of that envy still lingers in the passion for the precinct. And does Australia, also of the 'New World', somehow share that envy? Or on the other hand, is there perhaps an equally misleading envy of the new?

Let us take two examples. Cultural precincts as a concept follow naturally enough upon the idea of the arts festival, since both were mid-twentieth century artificial creations driven by the 'we need to do something' mentality of the day. In the UK they were both outcomes of the post-Blitz rebuild and the new Bevanite slum clearance housing estates that came to such social grief—the Milton Keynes of the arts, if you will. In Australia we took over, largely unthinkingly, the British model for Arts Councils and Festivals, ignoring that the first suited a unitary government rather than a federation and that the second was an attempt to respond to a war-blighted urban terrain. It is worth remembering that both Southbank and the Festival of Britain in 1951 celebrated the end of wartime rationing. Australia had virtually none of that, but we followed the piper anyway.

On the other side of the Atlantic, in the late 1970s when the precinct process began, many US cities were feeling the post-industrial blight represented by the 'brownfields' of the old abandoned urban cores. Nationwide in 1977 an estimated 400,000 to 600,000 such brownfields existed.[49] The arts, and crucially *building* for the arts, seemed to be the answer. Australia did not share this brownfield phenomenon, just as it did not share the British post-war ruin, but again we followed the leader. True, we had a flight from the cities to the suburbs, but our CBDs flourished, albeit soullessly with office towers. The inner radius, while depressed, was never deserted; and at the very time when the brownfields disaster struck the US, in Australia the Paddingtons, Fitzroys, Carltons and Balmains were beginning to be gentrified.

For good or ill, in the late twentieth century we have been a nation of imitators—of language, fashion, entertainment and so much else. In the late twentieth-century we even adopted the outward signs of protest. In the late nineteenth and early twentieth-century, Australia had a home-grown political protest movement, but by the 1960s we had adopted an almost entirely American version, including its patois. So did we, equally mindlessly, adopt a response to an urban problem that wasn't really there? Did we then also, robotically, take on cultural precincts as an apparent solution to it? And are we doing so still?

Whatever may be the case, by the turn of the century more than ninety American cities had plans to develop a cultural district. To give some idea of the enthusiasm which drove this endeavour and which it is fair to say has continued to drive it both here and increasingly among our northern neighbours, I quote from a publication of that period. It gives some sense of why, in subsequent decades, authorities both private and public have bought the argument. As well, it shows how generally low in the order of priority is any real concern for artistic or cultural achievement. Bear in mind that this publication was produced not by some institute of realtors but the eminently respectable institution Americans for the Arts:

> *The number of events in the Pittsburgh Cultural District increased from 250 in 1986 to nearly 600 in 1994, with audiences doubling to more than one million annually. In its first decade of operation, the district generated $33 million in public investment and $63 million in private and philanthropic funds, which in turn triggered $115 million in commercial activity [...] Three years after establishing the Tucson Arts District, 26 of the 112 businesses in the Arts District were new, 54% had increased their sales volume and 53% made renovations with an average cost of $105,000 each.*[50]

As to whether any of these might have happened anyway or in different circumstances is characteristically never tested or, to be fair, may now simply be untestable. It is perhaps not for nothing that elsewhere in this and other publications these districts are referred to as 'consumption compounds'. It all sounds vaguely fascist or at the very least, penal.

Contrary to these hopes, it seems the opposite has happened in the US. City leaders were so intent on remedying the downtown desert, which they mostly failed to do, that in the process, like the Romans of old, they created a (suburban) wilderness and called it peace. Generally we have done much the same in Australia, as Ross Elliott observes:

> *My question is now whether we haven't forgotten the importance of supporting and nurturing our suburban economies and our suburban communities: have we become preoccupied with cutting yet more ribbons on projects of inner city fiscal largesse?*[51]

He goes on to point out that suburbs are where nearly all of us live and actually work (85-90 per cent of Australian jobs are in suburban locations) and mainly play, and yet most governments remain overwhelmingly focussed on resourcing what happens in the capital city CBDs. He is not of course alone in making that complaint, but it does clarify the folly of our imitative obsession with the cultural precinct.

It is interesting to note that Sydney, which has been the capital least preoccupied with downtown 'precincts', has some six flourishing suburban arts centres ringing the metropolitan area. The recently announced move of the Powerhouse Museum of Applied Arts and Sciences to Parramatta might suggest that someone has taken note of the problem and is seeking to make some greater change. Yet it is noteworthy, too, that among the denunciations of that move by those once known as arts 'tsars' is the argument that the museum qua museum is solely an urban activity. It is as well the Guggenheim in Bilbao was not swayed by similar arguments.

Economics or otherwise

So is it all a case of mistaken identity? Is it the deep down recognition that many of the artistic and social claims made about the benefits of cultural precincts may be mistaken at heart? Perhaps this is why the economic justification has loomed so large since the 1980s in support of these developments. From the beginning, in the US these were seen as the reason to make the investments—beautify and animate cities; provide employment; attract residents and tourists to the city (i.e. the CBD); complement adjacent businesses; enhance property values; expand the tax base; attract well-educated employees; and, right at the tail, contribute to a creative, innovative environment. Even when they come to discuss the cultural institutions themselves, the measurements are in terms of increased seats sold and increased numbers of programs and events, which are all very fine, but no one seemed prepared to argue for better art or more challenging artists. Indeed, when attention turns to housing artists (as against housing the arts) we read such unlovely usages as the precinct's having a 'cultural production focus'. In this, the attraction is less in luring visitors than attracting residents but again there is little sense of what the benefit may be other than their presence. It is as though there was an odour of sanctity surrounding artists sufficient to culturally incense the district.

Since so many of the arguments for cultural precincts rely on economic or at the very least commercial claims, it is important to ask how much are these worth? On the face of it, given the available evidence, some rest on shaky ground. There are telling observations in some recent research on the matter. This looked at claims, such as those above, that the arts and cultural sector can boost productivity in other sectors of a local economy through creating urban environments that attract professionals with high levels of human capital along with their innovative, high-growth employers, as well as supplying other parts of the local economy—in particular, commercial creative firms—with new ideas and skills that enhance innovation. Now it is true that clusters and precincts are not precisely the same but the implications are broadly comparable. The researchers noted that 'although these arguments have justified policies for creative place making, urban branding, and public investments in signature buildings and dedicated cultural districts', the evidence base underpinning them is still sparse and mostly confined to the US. They set out to test this by 'building an econometric model exploring the impact of cultural clusters on the productivity of English cities largely through the impact of cultural agglomeration on worker wages at the city level'.[52] And what did they find?

First, there is evidence that skilled workers sacrifice

higher wages to locate in areas with strong cultural clustering. However, once they were

> *controlled for individual characteristics (particularly skills as proxied by an individual's qualifications), the coefficients for two out of our three measures of cultural clustering in our wage equations (cultural employment and institutions) become significantly negative, while the cultural occupations coefficient becomes insignificant.*[53]

In plain English: the only measurable change was minimal or negative.

Creative cities seem to be more productive, the study found, but only if we eliminate the rather obvious factor that affluent cities attract creative industries. Perhaps, they shyly suggest, it might be better to target occupations rather than industries if you want to push urban development. There is 'evidence of innovation spillovers [sic] from cultural clusters into the commercial creative economy' but here again, the researchers urge caution since (wonder of wonders) maybe a vibrant arts and cultural scene will emerge in places with more productive creative clusters. In other words, back to the drawing board. After all that, their tentative conclusion is that, although English data support the view that there is a relationship between cultural clustering and urban development, that relationship 'appears to be subtler than is generally acknowledged'. What was that about a mountain labouring?

These doubts are not new. Fifteen years earlier, some

experts were urging caution as much about the social benefits as the economic:

> *For example, a cultural district will effect urban renewal although it may create problems with gentrification. [...] To some the forcing out of economically disadvantaged citizens may hardly seem an improvement. The impacts of economic growth are even more uncertain. Indeed a regression analysis of six American cities over 17 years (during which each implemented a cultural district) reveals that the presence of a cultural district is actually associated (statistically significantly) with lower than average growth, even when controlling for population, time and the individual city effects. This may be as a result of the fact that cultural districts are often used as a strategy to fight existing growth problems, nonetheless the evidence of the efficacy of cultural districts in meeting this objective is hardly convincing.*[54]

That the cities in question were as widespread and wildly diverse as Boston, Charlotte, Dallas, Pittsburgh (lauded earlier) and Denver only makes this observation more striking.

However, just as I have argued that we should not have slavishly copied those modes of cultural practice from the US and UK, so I must equally acknowledge that these negative cases cannot be willy nilly applied to Australian conditions. The fact is we don't know, and that in itself is a concern.

Summing up

So what out of all this do I think?

I would argue that governments should intervene in this delicate market not by building more Towers of Babel but rather using the powers they have to leverage property development for arts and cultural purposes. Given the demographics of our societies, that can as readily apply to suburban areas as metropolitan CBDs. In the process they might save a lot of money that could be put to better cultural use.

- Consistent with this, the arts and cultural institutions need to be more imaginative about where they seek to locate themselves and perhaps a little less nervous of the market which they often purport to disdain without bothering to understand.
- Governments should aim to place their efforts where the people are and where they go, not to invest where the people are not in the hope of 'urban renewal'. In that respect, relocating resources to suburban centres may be the better path.
- I would urge that everyone stop crediting the false prophets of the Precinct church who are not delivering the goods to the arts but are merely profiting others who give little or nothing in return, *pace* Mr Packer.

Above all, arts organisations need to resist the trend to be corralled into predetermined government-ordained premises. This may be hard to do since the trend is now so ubiquitous that it is not just precincts but what might loosely be called 'arts houses' where publicly funded companies are being told in effect where they may live and are as a result stacked in cultural dovecotes that often seem more instruments of control than of residence.

And finally that we should recognise that in all of these cases, even where the authorities in question may be—and let's suppose are—well intentioned, they may not in fact be right.

Endnotes

1 Arthur C. Brooks and Roland Kushner, 'Cultural Districts and Urban Development', *International Journal of Arts Management,* Vol 3 No 2 (Winter 2001), p.6.
2 *Melbourne Arts Precinct Blueprint,* February 2014. http://creative.vic.gov.au/files/ea1c6732-f4f6-4c04-b8c0-a2d0012231f0/Melbourne_Arts_Precinct_Blueprint.pdf
3 Professor Sumner Miller was an American physicist who hosted a popular science program of the same name on ABC TV from 1963 to 1988.
4 Ien Ang & Fazal Rizvi, 'Precariously at Home: Chinatown in Sydney, Australia in Asia', *RUPC #2 / Surpllus #13.2,* Melbourne, Surpllus Pty Ltd 2013, p.5.
5 Henry James, *Italian Hour,* Auckland: The Floating Press 2010, p.342.
6 'Design Excellence: Cultural Precinct Plans', *Connecting Sydney's Cultural Jigsaw,* City Talks, 2 September 2014. http://www.cityofsydney.nsw.gov.au/council/news-and-updates/global-issues-ideas-and-conversations/city-talks-design/cultural-precinct-planning-connecting-sydneys-cultural-jigsaw
7 See Arts Queensland, *Queensland Cultural Precinct – Draft Master Plan,* Department of Science, Information Technology Innovation and the Arts, 2 April 2014. http://www.arts.qld.gov.au/docs/2%20APRIL%202014%20DRAFT%20CULTURAL%20PRECINCT%20MASTER%20PLAN%20DRAFT%20LOW%20RES.pdf
8 See Arts NSW, *Walsh Bay Arts Precinct Master Plan,* NSW Public Works, 6 August 2013. http://www.arts.nsw.gov.au/wp-content/uploads/2010/10/Walsh_bay-MP_201300806_A3_revG-1.pdf
9 e.g. *Project Rameau,* Sydney Dance Company in collaboration with Australian Chamber Orchestra, world premiere at Sydney Theatre, 29 October 2012.
10 *Newtown Cultural Quarter Project Two – Business Plan,* p.11. http://www.jda.org.za/keydocs/newtown/businessplan_newtownjuly2004.pdf
11 Regional Facilities Auckland, *Civic Administration Building: Three concepts for a thriving art and cultural precinct in the Aotea Quarter,* 2013. https://drive.google.com/file/d/0B0tiKSPbrSPNcy1NejZDa3NxYmc/view?pli=1
12 *see* http://www.gcdn.net/index/about-us/
13 Adrian Ellis, 'Successful cultural districts are powerful policy tools', *Comment,* Issue 248, July-August 2013. http://www.gcdn.net/index/about-us/
14 Adrian Ellis, http://www.gcdn.net/index/about-us/
15 Adrian Ellis.
16 Adrian Ellis.
17 Adrian Ellis.
18 Arthur C. Brooks and Roland Kushner, p.12.
19 John Armstrong, *In Search of Civilisation,* London: Penguin 2009, p.67.
20 The author should declare some interest in having been retained (after the event) to advise the Council on some of these aspects.

21 *Glimcher Retail Monitor*, http://www.wpglimcher.com/assets/newsarticles/pdfs/retail-survey-results-may-2013.pdf
22 *Glimcher Retail Monitor.*
23 *Glimcher Retail Monitor.*
24 Laurence Durrell, *Monsieur*, London: Faber & Faber 1974, p.282.
25 Laurence Durrell.
26 *see* Graeme Evans, 'From cultural quarters to creative clusters: creative spaces in the new city economy', *The sustainability and development of cultural quarters: International perspectives*, M. Legner & D. Ponzini (eds), Stockholm: Institute of Urban History 2009, pp.32-59.
27 Graeme Evans, 'From cultural quarters to creative clusters'.
28 Graeme Evans.
29 Graeme Evans.
30 Graeme Evans.
31 Australian Trade Commission, *Cultural Precincts*, July 2013. http://www.austrade.gov.au/ArticleDocuments/1358/Cultural-Precincts-ICR.pdf.aspx
32 *Melbourne Arts Precinct Blueprint*, February 2014, p.27. http://creative.vic.gov.au/files/ea1c6732-f4f6-4c04-b8c0-a2d0012231f0/Melbourne_Arts_Precinct_Blueprint.pdf
33 Leon van Schaik, 'Against another arts ghetto', *Arts Hub*, 17 February 2014. http://architecture.artshub.com.au/news-article/opinions-and-analysis/architecture/leon-van-schaik/against-another-arts-ghetto-198137
34 Leon van Schaik, 'Against another arts ghetto'.
35 Leon van Schaik.
36 Leon van Schaik.
37 Leon van Schaik.
38 Ben Eltham, 'Why Cultural Precincts Never Work', *Arts Hub*, 14 February 2014. http://www.artshub.com.au/news-article/features/trends-and-analysis/ben-eltham/why-cultural-precinct-plans-never-work-198108
39 Arts Queensland, 'An Urbis-led Partnership of Urbis, COX Rayner Architects and Lord Cultural Resources CULTURAL PRECINCT MASTER PLAN PROJECT NEWSLETTER #1—GETTING STARTED THE CULTURAL PRECINCT, SOUTH BANK', October 2013. http://arts.qld.gov.au/docs/CulturalPrecinctMP_ProjectNewsv2.pdf
40 Arts Queensalnd, 'An Urbis-led Partnrship of Ubis'.
41 Committee for Perth, 'Changing Face of Perth', *Insight e-newsletter*, Issue 46: February 2013. http://www.committeeforperth.com.au/pdf/Newsletters/insightFebruary2013.pdf
42 Committee for Perth, 'Changing Face of Perth'.
43 Committee for Perth, 'Changing Face of Perth'.
44 City of Gold Coast, *Gold Coast Cultural Precinct Vision Document.* http://www.goldcoastculturalprecinct.info/sites/default/files/vision2.pdf
45 City of Gold Coast, *Gold Coast Cultural Precinct Vision Document.*
46 *see* Wade Shepard, *Ghost Cities of China*, London: Zed Books 2015.
47 Patrick Brzeski, 'China to Create $800 Million Tax-Free Entertainment, Culture Hub in Beijing', *The Hollywood Reporter*, 22 March 2013.
48 Adrian Ellis.
49 Hilary Anne Frost-Kumpf, *Cultural Districts, The Arts as a Strategy for Revitalizing Our Cities*, Americans for the Arts 1998, p.5. http://www.americansforthearts.org/sites/default/files/Cultural%20Districts_0.pdf
50 Hilary Anne Frost-Kumpf, *Cultural Districts*, p.7.
51 Ross Elliott, 'Is it time for suburban renewal?', *On Line Opinion—Australia's e-journal of social and political debate*, 10 February 2015. http://www.onlineopinion.com.au/view.asp?article=17078&page=0

52 Hasan Bakhshi, Neil Lee and Juan Mateos Garcia, 'Capital of culture? An econometric analysis of the relationship between arts and cultural clusters, wages and the creative economy in English cities', *Nesta Working Paper,* No. 14/06, August 2014. https://www.nesta.org.uk/sites/default/files/1406_capital_of_culture_-_final.pdf

53 Hasan Bakhshi, Neil Lee and Juan Mateos Garcia, 'Capital of culture?

54 Arthur C. Brooks and Roland Kushner, p.12.

Copyright Information

PLATFORM PAPERS
Quarterly essays from Currency House Inc.
Founding Editor: Dr John Golder
Currency House Inc. is a non-profit association and resource centre advocating the role of the performing arts in public life by research, debate and publication.

Postal address: PO Box 2270, Strawberry Hills, NSW 2012, Australia
Email: info@currencyhouse.org.au Tel: (02) 9319 4953
Website: www.currencyhouse.org.au Fax: (02) 9319 3649

Editorial Committee: Katharine Brisbane AM, Michael Campbell, Dr Robin Derricourt, Professor Julian Meyrick, Martin Portus, Dr Nick Shimmon, Greig Tillotson

Cultural Precincts: Art or commodity? © Justin Macdonnell 2015

Except as permitted under the Copyright Act 1968, no part of this book may be reproduced without written permission. For details of the Copyright Agency Ltd licence, under the Act, for educational institutions, please contact CAL at info@copyright.com.au.

ISBN 978-0-9924890-5-2
ISSN 1449-583X

Typeset in Garamond
Printed by Lightning Source
Production by XOU Creative

FORTHCOMING

PP 45, November 2015
PAYING THE PIPER: THERE HAS TO BE A BETTER WAY
Cathy Hunt

In 2008 arts strategist Cathy Hunt, with UK researcher Phyllida Shaw, tackled arts structures and funding in Platform Papers 15, *A Sustainable Arts Sector: What will it take?*

In this paper she brings us new insights and findings to the topic.

In 2013 the newly-elected Queensland Government made budget cuts across the public sector resulting in the loss of around 14,000 jobs. In the arts it was the method as much as the numbers that raised questions. Why was the focus on the small to medium sector? Why was the Youth Arts sector hardest hit? And why no coordinated response from the sector as a whole?

Hunt uses the experience and its aftermath, including the recent decision by the Federal Minister to create the National Programme for Excellence in the Arts, to look more widely at the state of the arts today. Is the sector any closer to future proofing itself and what really needs to happen to make the vagaries of government funding schemes less significant in the evolution and development of a thriving cultural ecology.

AT YOUR LOCAL BOOKSHOP FROM 1 NOVEMBER
AND AS A PAPERBACK OR ON LINE
FROM OUR WEBSITE AT
WWW.CURRENCYHOUSE.ORG.AU

Printed in Australia
AUOC02n0834080715
268742AU00003B/3/P

9 780992 489052